BEYOND
Sunday

BEYOND

Sunday

*Becoming a
24/7 Catholic*

STUDY GUIDE

TERESA TOMEO AND GAIL CONIGLIO

**Our
Sunday
Visitor**

www.osv.com
Our Sunday Visitor Publishing Division
Our Sunday Visitor, Inc.
Huntington, Indiana 46750

Our Sunday Visitor Publishing Division
Our Sunday Visitor, Inc.
200 Noll Plaza
Huntington, IN 46750
1-800-348-2440

ISBN: 978-1-68192-227-0
Inventory No. X1930
Cover and interior design: Lindsey Riesen
Cover art: Shutterstock

PRINTED IN THE UNITED STATES OF AMERICA

Contents

YOUR BEYOND *Sunday* **STUDY GROUP** 6

WEEK ONE 11
Outside the Box: *Taking Faith Beyond Our Comfort Zone*

WEEK TWO 15
The Church as Field Hospital

WEEK THREE 19
"Late Have I Loved You": *We're Not the Only
Ones Taking the Long Way Home*

WEEK FOUR 23
Conscience and the American Catholic

WEEK FIVE 27
Up Close and Personal: *The Church and God in Our Everyday Lives*

WEEK SIX 31
The Three M's of Faith: *Meeting, Mercy, and Mission*

WEEK SEVEN 35
Five Cures for the Common Catholic Cold

WEEK EIGHT 39
"God Gives Us What We Need Wrapped in What We Want"

WRAP-UP 43
So Now What?

ABOUT THE AUTHORS 47

YOUR BEYOND *Sunday* STUDY GROUP

I. How to Get the Most out of This Study

You get out of something what you put into it. You've already taken the huge step of starting this Beyond Sunday journey, and we're excited to be on the way with you. This study guide is designed to help you live your faith "beyond Sunday" in your everyday life, with a community of people seeking the growth in faith alongside you. This study guide offers insights, personal stories, relevant examples, and plenty of fodder for group discussion as you seek to make your faith part of your daily life.

Below are some suggestions to help you get the most out of this study:

➜ Make your best effort to attend every class. If for some reason you need to miss, contact your facilitator and let him or her know you will not be there. Then, do the assigned workbook lesson for that week. You can even call or meet with your facilitator if you would like to share what you have learned and your Holy Habit plan for that week.

➜ Keep what you hear in the group meeting confidential. Do not share what you hear with anyone — it's important to avoid sharing information other people would rather keep private, and, of course, we want to avoid gossip. This group should be a safe place for sharing with honesty and vulnerability. It's important for everyone to recognize that we've all sinned and fallen short — and that's why we need one another to help keep us accountable.

➜ Read the recommended readings for each week before each group meeting and write down your answers to all of the reflection questions openly and honestly.

➜ We encourage you to take notes during your personal reading and in the group meetings, during the video either in the "notes" section at the end of each session or in a separate notebook or journal.

➜ Take the time to explore the resources (located in the Beyond Sunday appendix).

➜ If you haven't been to the Sacrament of Reconciliation in a long time (or especially if not within the past year), we highly recommend that you make the effort to get right with God so that any barriers of sin don't cloud your heart and mind from Christ Jesus.

➜ Forgive others who have hurt you. Harboring unforgiveness can hold us back from receiving all of the graces God has for us. Make a list of those you need to forgive and ask God to help you forgive them.

➜ If you find this study helpful (and we pray you will!), tell someone about it and encourage him or her to try it out if they're seeking to give their own faith life a boost.

➜ Even after the study ends, go back and revisit the Holy Habits of the Week, the prayers, and your own notes. This occasional review will help you to continue to grow in your faith and in your relationship with Jesus Christ.

II. Tips for a Successful Small Group Study

While this is set up as an eight-week study, consider holding ten total meetings: an introduction meeting where you will review the themes, pray, hand out materials, and do some icebreakers to get to know one another; eight meetings corresponding to each chapter in the *Beyond Sunday* book; and a final meeting to do a wrap-up, cover the Beyond Sunday resources, field any follow-up questions, and perhaps hold a celebration social with time for fellowship and sharing. You can open your group to share any testimonies of what they received from this study.

→ Select a Beyond Sunday coordinator for your parish.

→ Reserve well in advance the room/space where you will be meeting.

→ Personal invitation is key. Invite friends, family members, coworkers, or fellow parishioners to join the study group.

→ Promote your Beyond Sunday study in the parish bulletin, online, and anywhere your parish offers space for small group promotion.

→ Make a participant list and ask permission to share it with the group.

→ Confidentiality is a must! Keep what you hear in the group strictly confidential.

→ Start and end your group meetings on time. Assign a timekeeper for each section to assure you will get through the entire lesson on time. Timing guidelines are listed next to each item in this study.

→ Although the study group format is sixty minutes, assign ninety minutes to the study to allow time before and afterward for fellowship.

→ Invite your parish priest or deacon to the first and last class, asking him to give you a special blessing for each.

→ Serving refreshments during the study is welcoming. Consider having a sign-up sheet so participants can sign up to bring refreshments, if appropriate, for the place where you are meeting. This will encourage fellowship and help build Christian friendships and the community.

→ Stay away from tangents. Keep your group on track and bring them back when they start going off-topic.

→ Schedule a follow-up study or fellowship gathering with your Beyond Sunday group participants.

→ Consider printing up Beyond Sunday graduation certificates and having a graduation ceremony where your parish priest attends and participants can give testimony to their growth through this study. Contact BeyondSunday@osv.com for more information on how to obtain these certificates.

III. Tips for Promoting Your Beyond Sunday Study

➜ Put notices in the bulletin at least four weeks prior to the group starting. Have the bulletin promotion run weekly for at least four weeks.

➜ Post about your group on social media. If your parish has a Facebook page, consider investing in low-cost advertising to promote your post to those that follow you.

➜ Make personal phone calls to other study group leaders, asking them to invite others they know to join the Beyond Sunday group.

➜ Make fliers and posters, and put them around the church.

➜ Send invitations about Beyond Sunday to the various groups in the parish as well as CCD and Catholic-school parents.

➜ Make phone calls and/or send emails to parish ministry leaders, asking them to invite and forward this information to their respective groups.

➜ Make a pulpit announcement at the end of Mass, sharing a short, two-minute testimony about how going "beyond Sunday" can change us as individuals and change the world. At the end of your testimony invite parishioners to sign-up for the next study and give registration and start dates.

➜ Set up a table with sign-up sheets in the back of the church and have someone there after all weekend Masses. Encourage others to join the study group, and answer any questions people have.

➜ Consider inviting Teresa Tomeo and Gail Coniglio to offer a parish mission at your parish. This is the most effective way to get a Beyond Sunday group going at your parish. Teresa and Gail would speak at all Masses on a given weekend, train your facilitators, and encourage parishioners to join in this much-needed study. To invite Teresa and Gail to your parish, email **beyondsunday@osv.com**.

IV. Small Group Weekly Meeting Suggested Format
(for suggested sixty-minute study)

→ Start with the opening prayer (3 minutes).

→ Have someone read the reflection out loud (3 minutes).

→ Have someone read the Beyond Sunday Brother/Sister out loud (3 minutes).

→ Give the participants time to answer the reflection questions (10 minutes).

→ Play the video and take any notes and write them in the NOTES section (5 minutes).

→ Give the participants time to answer the video reflection question (5 minutes).

→ Open up your group to sharing (15 minutes).

→ Discuss the week's Holy Habits and invite the group to talk about other ideas for living faith beyond Sunday (10 minutes).

→ Remind everyone of the date of the next class and the recommended reading for that class (1 minute).

→ End with the suggested closing prayer and intercessions (5 minutes).

Outside the Box
Taking Faith Beyond Our Comfort Zone

....

"Get comfortable with being uncomfortable."

— JIM HARBAUGH, HEAD FOOTBALL COACH, UNIVERSITY OF MICHIGAN

Let Us Pray

Lord, help me take my faith out of my comfort zone. If I've been keeping it in a comfortable box, help me to take it out and begin to live it fully.

Holy Spirit Prayer

Come, Holy Spirit, fill the hearts of your faithful and kindle in us the fire of your love.

Send forth your Spirit and we shall be created.

And you shall renew the face of the earth.

Let us pray.

O God, who by the light of the Holy Spirit did instruct the hearts of the faithful,

grant that by the same Holy Spirit we may be truly wise and ever enjoy his consolations.

Through Christ our Lord. Amen.

BEYOND *Sunday* REFLECTION

University of Michigan coach Jim Harbaugh knows a lot about life and about what it takes to be a person of integrity, and he applies that knowledge to his coaching. More importantly, he is a devout Catholic who loves and lives his faith. This coach is definitely teaching his players to go outside their comfort zone — to push and work a little harder if they want to be successful on and off the field. As a matter of fact, he often tells team members they need to "get comfortable with being uncomfortable." Imagine that! Harbaugh wants his players to learn that success, happiness, fulfillment, and growth don't come without some (or much) discomfort. As the saying goes, no pain, no gain. This holds true even when we start a new exercise routine.

Let's face it. We're living in what has become, for the most part, a post-Christian culture. Christians, especially Catholic Christians, who take their faith seriously are not exactly the most popular people on Facebook, on Twitter, at the office, or even in the local parish. Church teachings tend to run directly counter to the hot-button issues of our day. The Church also challenges us to dig deeper into our faith, to be willing to be comfortable with being uncomfortable for the sake of our own salvation, and to help build a better world.

When people who are successful and famous tell us to challenge or stretch ourselves, we believe it, and we often try to emulate it — at least when it comes to sports, business, or earning that extra degree or certificate to help us move forward in life. We love those feel-good, rags-to-riches stories of folks overcoming obstacles. We often have a hard time, however, applying this mentality to our faith journey. Why is that?

Could it be because deep down we know that getting comfortable with being uncomfortable in our life of faith means more than temporary discomfort — it means a radical change in our values and our life?

Leaving Jesus in a neat little box is so much easier. But taking our faith outside of that box, while certainly challenging at times, doesn't mean a life of constant misery and struggle. Actually, it is quite the opposite! If we leave our faith in a neat little box, we will never be truly happy, and we will never know the true peace and joy God wants to give us.

Having a successful business plan or a winning football team is great, but if you want to score big for eternity, let God truly be your life's coach. Ask him to help you get comfortable with being uncomfortable — both on and off the playing field.

Catechism Connection

"Coming to see in the faith their new dignity, Christians are called to lead henceforth a life 'worthy of the gospel of Christ.' They are made capable of doing so by the grace of Christ and the gifts of his Spirit, which they receive through the sacraments and through prayer.

"Following Christ and united with him, Christians can strive to be 'imitators of God as beloved children, and walk in love' by conforming their thoughts, words and actions to the 'mind … which is yours in Christ Jesus,' and by following his example.

"'Justified in the name of the Lord Jesus Christ and in the Spirit of our God,' 'sanctified … [and] called to be saints,' Christians have become the temple of the *Holy Spirit*. This 'Spirit of the Son' teaches them to pray to the Father and, having become their life, prompts them to act so as to bear 'the fruit of the Spirit' by charity in action. Healing the wounds of sin, the Holy Spirit renews us interiorly through a spiritual transformation. He enlightens and strengthens us to live as 'children of light' through 'all that is good and right and true.'" (CCC 1692, 1694–99)

This Week's "Beyond Sunday" Brother

Jim Harbaugh, University of Michigan head football coach

"The role that (faith) plays in my life is in the priorities that I have: faith, then family, then football." This is not something you would hear ESPN or your local sports radio station discussing when covering the Michigan Wolverines. But Jim Harbaugh has his priorities in order.

He spoke with the Catholic News Agency following a general audience with Pope Francis in April 2017, telling the news outlet how thrilled he was that he and his wife had the opportunity to meet Pope Francis and present him with a University of Michigan helmet and cleats. The coach also recognizes the importance of helping his family and his players to get outside the box when it comes to learning about life.

"Not all learning is done in a classroom or on the football field, you know? It's out connecting with people, and having a chance for our players and staff to see things they've never seen before, eat things they've never tasted, to hear a language they've never heard." Harbaugh also referenced the Bible, more specifically, 2 Timothy 4:7, in which Saint Paul talks about our life of faith in terms of sports: "Strive hard to win the prize, to have that motivation, to have that quality of perseverance and discipline and drive is what makes a really good athlete."

It's game time. Get out of your comfort zone and try something new. Don't stand on the sidelines and let faith pass you by. The more you focus and keep your eye on the ball, the more you will be able to move toward the goal. The more you participate, the closer you will get to reaching the winning prize — eternal life in heaven with God.

❓ Reflection Questions

1. How comfortable are you today with living your faith in your daily life, beyond Sunday?

2. Is there something in particular when it comes to practicing (or sharing) your faith that makes you feel uncomfortable? If so, what is that something, and why do you think it makes you uncomfortable?

3. What is one activity you could do to help you go outside your comfort zone and stretch yourself for Christ? (Here are some examples: sharing your faith with a friend or coworker, joining a Bible study, praying with your spouse, praying the Rosary, going to daily Mass, volunteering to read at church, teaching religious education/CCD, visiting a nursing home, contacting an estranged friend or family member, volunteering at a local pregnancy crisis center.)

4. Are there any obstacles holding you back from taking on this activity? What are they?

5. What are some concrete steps you can take on this week to help you overcome any obstacles that are keeping you from going out of your comfort zone?

▶ Video Reflection

Watch and reflect on the Beyond Sunday "Outside the Box" video, available at **www.OSV.com/BeyondSunday**. Spend some time discussing it with your group. What did you relate to most in the video and why?

👤 Holy Habits of the Week

→ Shake up your faith routine by doing something different this week. Maybe that will mean praying grace before every meal, even when eating out at a restaurant, or making note of one point that strikes you in the homily at Mass this week and sharing with a friend or family member.

→ Challenge yourself to do something uncomfortable for Jesus. It could be as simple as putting a holy card in a prominent place in your office, no matter what anyone else might think or say.

✝ Closing Prayer: *Act of Faith*

O my God, I firmly believe that you are one God in three divine Persons, Father, Son, and Holy Spirit. I believe that your divine Son became man and died for our sins and that he will come to judge the living and the dead. I believe these and all the truths which the Holy Catholic Church teaches because you have revealed them who are eternal truth and wisdom, who can neither deceive nor be deceived. In this faith I intend to live and die. Amen.

Close the meeting with a prayer of intercession, inviting everyone to pray for the needs of their community.

Read Chapter Two in the *Beyond Sunday* book before your next Beyond Sunday group meeting.

Notes

The Church as Field Hospital

....

"Faith by itself, if it has no works, is dead."

— JAMES 2:17

Let Us Pray

Lord, open our eyes and give us courage to look at the causes behind our "faith fallouts." Help us to give you permission to diagnose our common Catholic ailments and take the necessary actions to prevent them in the future.

Holy Spirit Prayer

Come, Holy Spirit, fill the hearts of your faithful and kindle in us the fire of your love.

Send forth your Spirit and we shall be created.

And you shall renew the face of the earth.

Let us pray.

O God, who by the light of the Holy Spirit did instruct the hearts of the faithful,

grant that by the same Holy Spirit we may be truly wise and ever enjoy his consolations.

Through Christ our Lord. Amen.

BEYOND *Sunday* REFLECTION

Use it or lose it. No doubt you've heard this expression before. We often hear it regarding our mental and physical fitness. We need to exercise our brains and our bodies to keep in shape, and if we don't, we pay the price.

Physically, as we're all too well aware, there is a huge amount of research showing what happens when we let ourselves become couch potatoes. Most of us would probably much rather be sitting on the sofa with a glass of vino in one hand and a big box of Cheez-Its in the other, not heading to the gym or taking a brisk walk. But if we don't get up and use the healthy bodies we've been given, we'll lose that health and vitality. And it's the same with our mental abilities. If we don't study and keep our minds active, we'll lose much of what we've learned.

Both our mind and body would pretty much turn to mush — or in other words, we would "lose it" — if we never exercised them. If we don't use our minds and bodies properly, we lose their proper functions and end up with illnesses such as heart disease, diabetes, or dementia.

The same holds true for our spiritual life if we don't keep it in shape. As Teresa described in Chapter 2 of the *Beyond Sunday* book, that's how she ended up with severe cases of Only on Sunday Syndrome, Christeritis, and many other common Catholic ailments. She was a "couch potato Christian," so to speak. We all run the risk of developing various spiritual sicknesses if we don't exercise our souls as routinely as we do our bodies and minds.

Using our bodies and minds to their fullest potential is a way to live a healthier and more productive life. In a similar way, putting our faith into action through our efforts to get to know Jesus more personally and to make a difference in the world will yield tons of good fruit, help us to experience peace beyond all understanding in difficult times throughout this life, and help us cross that finish line to heaven. Receiving the sacraments as frequently as possible is a great way to keep spiritually fit.

Participating in this study is also a way you can get moving in your faith life beyond Sunday. We encourage you to participate fully in the Monday-through-Saturday tips at the end of each chapter, which will help you to put your faith into action each week. This will help you stay in spiritual shape and shed some of your old habits that may be weighing you down and keeping you from connecting with God.

If your time is limited this week, be sure at least to read the "Good and Bad Habits" section of www .UnleashTheGospel.org pastoral letter by Archbishop Allen H. Vigneron of Detroit

 Catechism Connection

"Jesus' invitation to enter his kingdom comes in the form of *parables*, a characteristic feature of his teaching. Through his parables he invites people to the feast of the kingdom, but he also asks for a radical choice: to gain the kingdom, one must give everything. Words are not enough; deeds are required. The parables are like mirrors for man: will he be hard soil or good earth for the word? What use has he made of the talents he has received?" (CCC 546)

This Week's "Beyond Sunday" Sister
Saint Catherine of Siena

"Love does not stay idle."

If you start reading up on Saint Catherine of Siena (and you should!), you might begin to wonder why we picked her for this study guide chapter on common Catholic ailments. She was not exactly a spiritual slouch or faith couch potato during her life, and she's been named a Doctor of the Church, which means her witness and work are of great importance in terms of theology and Church doctrine.

Catherine is best known for her *Dialogue*, a book she wrote that details her dialogue with God. She had visions of God from the time she was a young girl, and she wanted nothing more than to be in solitude with the one she loved so passionately and to whom she was so strongly connected. But God had other plans. When she was twenty-one years old, Catherine had a vision of Jesus, who told her to go out into the world to serve the poor. It's not what she wanted. She would much rather have stayed in her room where she could privately commune with Christ.

Following God's plan is not always what we expect or want at first. These feelings are not uncommon, and you are in good company if you're encountering this in your walk with God. If such a great saint struggled with these feelings, it is natural that we will too.

But Saint Catherine knew that faith demands that we act according to God's will, so despite her discomfort, she did what the Lord asked. In addition to serving the poor and others in need, she also became a political activist in her day, writing letters to various rulers and religious leaders calling on them to work for peace. Not only did she refuse to be a spiritual couch potato herself, she worked tirelessly to make sure the leaders of the Church in her day were taking care of their own spiritual health and that of the whole Church. She even wrote letters encouraging the pope to take politically unpopular action that was needed for the good of the Church. Even a smile and saying, "Thank you, Father, for your great homily," after church on Sunday can make all the difference in the day in your parish priest.

We should keep Saint Catherine in mind, especially in these tumultuous times in which we are living. The Church is continually under attack. Putting your faith into action is neither popular nor easy. In fact, you may even get criticized for it. But don't get discouraged. Even the smallest actions or gestures that lift another person that are done with courage and love can go a long way.

❓ Reflection Questions

1. Take a look in that spiritual mirror and revisit the list of Common Catholic Ailments in Chapter 2 of the *Beyond Sunday* book. Which of them might apply to your faith life right now?

2. What causes, situations, challenges, etc., in your life helped bring this ailment on?

3. Is the ailment (or are the ailments) also common among your circle of friends and family? What can you do about curing this ailment?

4. Are there areas in your life where you could "use" your Catholic faith more fully, so you don't "lose" it?

▶ Video Reflection

Watch and reflect on the Beyond Sunday "Church as Field Hospital" video, available at **www.OSV.com/BeyondSunday**. Spend some time discussing it with your group. What did you relate to most in the video and why?

👤 Holy Habits of the Week

If we don't use it, we're likely to lose it. This week, let's exercise that spiritual muscle a little more than we usually do. Here are some ideas to help you practice your faith every day this week, aside from the weekly Mass obligation.

→ Pick two days this week and set your alarm for fifteen minutes earlier. You can spend that extra time in prayer or reading and reflecting on the Mass readings for that day. (See the Resources Appendix in the *Beyond Sunday* book.)

→ Has it been a while since you prayed the Rosary? Pick one evening this week, find a quiet corner in the house or go for a nice walk in your neighborhood, and spend twenty minutes saying the Rosary. You won't regret it! You can download a helpful pamphlet on how to say the Rosary at www.osv.com/Portals/4/documents/pdf/howtorosary.pdf or can visit www.ewtn.com/devotionals/prayers/rosary/how_to.htm to learn more about praying the Rosary.

→ Is there a crucifix displayed in a prominent place in your home? If not, consider finding one this week and hanging it in a room you and your family use often. Be sure the crucifix is blessed first by a priest.

→ Reflect on Matthew 7:16, "You will know them by their fruits." Which of the fruits of the Holy Spirit do you wish to have more of in your life — love, joy, peace, patience, kindness, generosity, faithfulness, gentleness, or self-control? Ask God to help you cultivate these good fruits.

✝ Closing Prayer: *Our Father*

Join as a group and say an Our Father very slowly together, considering every word.

Our Father, who art in heaven, hallowed be thy name. Thy Kingdom come. Thy will be done, on earth as it is in heaven. Give us this day our daily bread. And forgive us our trespasses, as we forgive those who trespass against us. And lead us not into temptation, but deliver us from evil. Amen.

Close the meeting with a prayer of intercession, inviting everyone to pray for the needs of their community.

• •

Read Chapter Three in the *Beyond Sunday* book before your next Beyond Sunday group meeting.

• •

Notes

"Late Have I Loved You"
We're Not the Only Ones Taking the Long Way Home

"Return to the LORD your God, / for he is gracious and merciful, / Slow to anger, and abounding in mercy."

— JOEL 2:13

Let Us Pray

Lord, help me realize how much you love me. Increase my faith in that love.

Holy Spirit Prayer

Come, Holy Spirit, fill the hearts of your faithful and kindle in us the fire of your love.

Send forth your Spirit and we shall be created.

And you shall renew the face of the earth.

Let us pray.

O God, who by the light of the Holy Spirit did instruct the hearts of the faithful,

grant that by the same Holy Spirit we may be truly wise and ever enjoy his consolations.

Through Christ our Lord. Amen.

BEYOND *Sunday* REFLECTION

Most of us feel lost sometimes. If we've been badly hurt by others or have suffered from our own mistakes, we may even be tempted to fear that we'll never be accepted, especially not in the Church. We can feel so unworthy that we avoid church and anything having to do with God, sometimes for years.

If you're feeling this way, or if you ever have, know that it doesn't matter where you've been or how long you've been away. When we turn to him, God always welcomes us with open arms. Even if we are already "home" by going to Mass regularly, is that home in the Church truly where our heart is?

A good way to get there is by revisiting the ABCs of mercy, highlighted in Chapter 3 of the *Beyond Sunday* book. We have to ask for God's mercy, we have to accept that mercy, and then we have to completely trust in him.

A great place to start in asking for mercy is the Sacrament of Reconciliation, more commonly known as confession. Don't worry if you haven't been there in a while; the priest will walk you through the steps. There is no need to be nervous about telling your sins to a priest; in the confessional, the priest is acting in the person of Christ, or *in persona Christi*. He's just a conduit of mercy, which comes directly from God. The Church wants all of us to believe fully that Christ forgives our sins through the ministry of his priests.

Secondly, be willing to extend mercy and forgiveness to others who have hurt you. The Our Father is a good prayer to say to help remind us that we've been forgiven and need to forgive likewise.

Finally, surrender to Jesus and ask him to help you trust him completely. When it comes to receiving God's mercy, there isn't some secret formula or prayer. You just need an open heart and a willingness to put God in the driver's seat. Try saying the simple prayer revealed to Saint Faustina, the apostle of divine mercy: "Jesus, I trust in you." Say it in the morning when you wake up, and again (if you can remember) at 3:00 in the afternoon, the hour of mercy.

Mercy isn't a one-time thing, either. We need God's mercy every day. We need to re-commit our lives every day to Christ. Once you practice these exercises, including making your way to confession, you will see that it's a lot simpler than you might have imagined.

 ## *Catechism* Connection

"'There is no one, however wicked and guilty, who may not confidently hope for forgiveness, provided his repentance is honest.' Christ who died for all men desires that in his Church the gates of forgiveness should always be open to anyone who turns away from sin." (CCC 982)

This Week's "Beyond Sunday" Brother
Singer-songwriter Dion DiMucci

"Catholicism gets in your DNA, and growing up with it, it gets into your bones, even when you are not going to church."

Dion DiMucci is probably best known for his years spent wandering, and that wandering is not just based on the song that helped propel him to the Rock and Roll Hall of Fame. Dion, of the famous Dion and the Belmonts, was raised in an Italian American Catholic family in the Bronx. Despite his Catholic upbringing, his talents as a singer and songwriter soon propelled him to fame and fortune and pulled him far away from God and the Church of his youth.

DiMucci's most famous hit was "The Wanderer," known to a lot of us because it's such a classic and also probably familiar to many millennials because the tune is used in Fallout 4, a popular video game. The money and attention he earned in the music world eventually got the best of him. Even though he had everything he thought he needed for happiness, he was empty. As a result, he became addicted to drugs and alcohol. Yet somewhere in the back of his mind, he recalled the words of his local parish priest back in New York, reminding him that seeking happiness through worldly success would leave him unfulfilled.

Finally, in a desperate attempt to turn his life around, he got on his knees and asked God for help. As DiMucci explains it, something happened after saying that prayer, and he was able to break free from his addictions.

He wandered for a while, in and out of different Christian denominations. He was reading Scripture and began to learn about the early saints and leaders in the Church. Their stories and a desire to receive Jesus in the Eucharist brought him back home to the Catholic Church in 1997.

DiMucci's story offers all of us a lot of hope. We can go home again and again, no matter where we've been or how long we've been gone. All it takes is a knee and a prayer.

❓ Reflection Questions

1. Do you struggle with feeling lovable and worthy of belonging in the Church?

2. How do you feel about this idea of "surrendering," turning your life to God, as Dion DiMucci did?

3. Are you comfortable asking God into (or back into) your life? If not, why not?

4. When was the last time you tapped into God's mercy in the sacrament of confession?

🧑 Holy Habits of the Week

→ Do a quick search on the internet for Scripture verses on the love of God. You'll quickly see there are dozens upon dozens to choose from. Select a few of them, and spend some time reflecting on just how much God loves you.

→ Consider praying three Hail Marys (one each for the Theological Virtues of Faith, Hope, and Charity) every morning when you start driving (to the office, to school, to run errands, etc.). You may even want to pray a decade of the Rosary.

▶ Video Reflection

Watch and reflect on the Beyond Sunday "Late Have I Loved You" video, available at **www.OSV.com /BeyondSunday**. Spend some time discussing it with your group. What did you relate to most in the video and why?

✝ Closing Prayer: *Pardon Prayer*

(taught by the Angel to the three children at Fátima, Portugal, in 1916)

"My God, I believe, I adore, I hope, and I love thee! I beg pardon for those who do not believe, do not adore, do not hope, and do not love thee." *(Repeat three times.)*

Close the meeting with a prayer of intercession, inviting everyone to pray for the needs of their community.

. . . .
Read Chapter Four in the *Beyond Sunday* book before your next Beyond Sunday group meeting.
. . . .

Notes

_____

_____

_____

_____

Notes

Conscience and the American Catholic

"If I am delayed, you may know how one ought to behave in the household of God, which is the Church of the living God, the pillar and bulwark of the truth."

— 1 Timothy 3:15

Let Us Pray

Lord, help us to form our consciences well. Let our conscience guide us to actions that will lead to true peace and fulfillment.

Holy Spirit Prayer

Come, Holy Spirit, fill the hearts of your faithful and kindle in us the fire of your love.

Send forth your Spirit and we shall be created.

And you shall renew the face of the earth.

Let us pray.

O God, who by the light of the Holy Spirit did instruct the hearts of the faithful,

grant that by the same Holy Spirit we may be truly wise and ever enjoy his consolations.

Through Christ our Lord. Amen.

BEYOND *Sunday* REFLECTION

During the presidential election of 2016, probably the most contentious and divisive in the history of the United States, Teresa received quite a few emails from listeners who wanted to explain why they were voting for particular candidates. In some cases, people were planning to vote for politicians who identify Catholicism as their chosen religion but whose vigorous support for certain actions stands in direct opposition to Church teaching, especially in the areas of human life and marriage.

One woman explained that she was comfortable with her decisions because most of her Catholic friends were voting the same way and because she had discussed it with them. While this can be a tempting way to think, just remember that question your mother probably asked you when you were a kid wanting to join the crowd, even though it violated parental rules and might have put you in harm's way: "If all the kids jumped off a bridge, would you jump too?"

Aside from talking to her friends about her decision, the woman made no mention of consulting her pastor, Scripture, resources such as the United States Conference of Catholic Bishops voter's guide, or the *Catechism*. It is very likely that the Holy Spirit was challenging this woman, which is why she wrote to Teresa in the first place. She was trying to justify her actions, and, since she found some friends who agreed with her, she thought that made everything okay.

A lot of us do the same thing, and far too often. Rather than seek to form our consciences according to the teachings of the Church, we seek out the reassurance of our friends that whatever we decide is just fine as long as it feels right. Yet if we take our faith seriously, we can't just set it aside during elections, or when we have to make difficult moral decisions. As a matter of fact, it should guide all of our decisions, including the way we vote. In other words, as a wise priest once said, "Our Catholic faith shouldn't be *a* factor when we go to the polls (or when we make any other significant choice), it should be *the* factor."

As Venerable Fulton Sheen expressed it: "The Catholic Church never suits any particular mood of any age. A Catholic knows that if the Church married the mood of any age in which it lived, it would be a widow in the next age. The mark of the true Church is that it will never get on well with the passing moods of the world." We can learn more about a particular truth over time, and when that happens we change; the truth does not.

The interesting thing is, in any situation other than those dealing with deep moral issues, folks rarely push for their own opinion as the standard of action. Would we do that with our jobs? Would we tell our bosses we don't like starting at 8 a.m., and that we'll be in at 10 or whenever we wake up and decide to get dressed? Would we tell the local gym that we don't like their hours so they need a different schedule to accommodate our lifestyle? Yet when it comes to truly listening to the Church on issues that matter most of all, we often don't take her teachings seriously. It's easier to believe that the rules don't apply and that we can go along making up our own.

Yet the Church is the pillar and foundation of truth. So if our decisions and actions don't line up with Scripture and Church teaching, we're following something other than the truth. We can claim all we want that we're following our conscience; that may be true, but if our conscience urges us to go against truth, then our conscience needs formation.

Catechism Connection

"Deep within his conscience man discovers a law which he has not laid upon himself but which he must obey. Its voice, ever calling him to love and to do what is good and to avoid evil, sounds in his heart at the right moment.… For man has in his heart a law inscribed by God.… His conscience is man's most secret core and his sanctuary. There he is alone with God whose voice echoes in his depths."

"It is important for every person to be sufficiently present to himself in order to hear and follow the voice of his conscience. This requirement of *interiority* is all the more necessary as life often distracts us from any reflection, self-examination or introspection." (CCC 1776, 1779, emphasis in original)

This Week's "Beyond Sunday" Brother
Saint Thomas More

"The clearness of my conscience has made my heart hop for joy."

Saint Thomas More (1478–1535) was a great scholar, writer, lawyer, politician, and a devoted Catholic. He was also knighted by King Henry VIII and eventually became one of the king's closest and most influential advisers. Saint Thomas worked tirelessly to defend the Catholic faith in England. His close relationship with the king became strained when he learned that Henry VIII was planning to break away from the Church in Rome. The king granted himself an annulment from his wife so he could marry Anne Boleyn. Saint Thomas refused to support the king's decision because he knew it was against Church teaching and made a mockery of marriage. As a result, he was locked in the Tower of London and eventually beheaded. He went to his death telling the world: "I die the king's good servant, but God's first."

Saint Thomas More shows us what a well-formed conscience looks like. Following our conscience can never mean going with the flow or conforming to the opinions of others. Instead, if we're really interested in the truth, we must conform our will to God's and the truths taught by his Church, no matter what.

❓ Reflection Questions

1. What does it mean that man "has in his heart a law inscribed by God"? How should we recognize and respond to what God has written on our hearts?

2. How do you personally work to form your conscience?

3. In what ways does life distract you from the necessary reflection and self-examination needed to form your conscience properly?

▶ Video Reflection

Watch and reflect on the Beyond Sunday "Conscience and the American Catholic" video, available at **www.OSV.com /BeyondSunday**. Spend some time discussing it with your group. What did you relate to most in the video and why?

👤 Holy Habits of the Week

→ This week think and pray about the process you've been using to make important moral decisions in your life. Take a look deep in your heart to see if you have truly been guided by the Holy Spirit and by the authoritative teachings of the Church.

→ Find and print out a short examination of conscience (see the resources in the Beyond Sunday appendix for links), and put it by your bedside. Spend two minutes examining your conscience each night, and then pray the Act of Contrition (see below).

✝ Closing Prayer: *Act of Contrition*

My God, I am sorry for my sins with all my heart. In choosing to do wrong and failing to do good, I have sinned against you whom I should love above all things.

I firmly intend, with your help, to do penance, to sin no more, and to avoid whatever leads me to sin. Our Savior Jesus Christ suffered and died for us. In his name, my God, have mercy.

Close the meeting with a prayer of intercession, inviting everyone to pray for the needs of their community.

. . . .

Read Chapter Five in the *Beyond Sunday* book before your next Beyond Sunday group meeting.

. . . .

Notes

_____

_____

_____

_____

Notes

Up Close and Personal
The Church and God in Our Everyday Lives

"O LORD, you have searched me and known me!"
— PSALMS 139:1

Let Us Pray

Lord, help us to live each day of our lives with meaning and purpose, always aiming to draw closer to you.

Holy Spirit Prayer

Come, Holy Spirit, fill the hearts of your faithful and kindle in us the fire of your love.

Send forth your Spirit and we shall be created.

And you shall renew the face of the earth.

Let us pray.

O God, who by the light of the Holy Spirit did instruct the hearts of the faithful,

grant that by the same Holy Spirit we may be truly wise and ever enjoy his consolations.

Through Christ our Lord. Amen.

BEYOND *Sunday* REFLECTION

God knows us better than we know ourselves because he created us in his image and likeness. If we could just grasp how well God knows us and how much he loves us, then the idea of a personal relationship with him wouldn't seem so foreign or unachievable.

If you're still trying to grasp this, grab your Bible (or your phone or laptop) and go to John 21:1–17. This Scripture passage, in which Jesus makes breakfast for his disciples on the shore of the Sea of Galilee, shows us just how personal God is and how he gives us what we need, not only to carry on but to be fishers of men. You're probably familiar with the story in general. But what a lot of us miss about Jesus' conversation with Peter is the importance of the charcoal fire. There they are, sitting around the fire on the beach, and eating fish cooked by Jesus. Seems like a pretty normal setting for the time.

However, it wasn't too long before that meeting on the seashore that Peter had been warming himself at another charcoal fire. That fire was in the courtyard of the high priest, and it was there that he denied Christ three times. To say Peter was filled with remorse and sadness over those denying Jesus outside the house of Caiaphas and over hiding during and after the Crucifixion would be a huge understatement. But instead of reminding Peter of what a coward he was, Jesus gives him another chance over a different charcoal fire. Three times Peter had denied Jesus, and now Jesus gives Peter the chance three times to redeem himself and start anew.

That's how up close and personal God wants to be for each and every one of us. Jesus met Peter where he was that day on the beach. Many of us think that our sins are unforgivable, but this story should give us great hope. Even Jesus' closest friend denied him three times. It is part of our fallen human nature to sin, which is why we need God's grace and mercy. We can trust that no one is out of God's reach. As Jesus told Saint Faustina, "The greater the sin, the greater the right he has to my mercy."

 ## *Catechism* Connection

"But St. John goes even further when he affirms that 'God is Love'; God's very being is love. By sending his only Son and the Spirit of Love in the fullness of time, God has revealed his innermost secret: God himself is an eternal exchange of love, Father, Son, and Holy Spirit, and he has destined us to share in that exchange." (CCC 221)

This Week's "Beyond Sunday" Brother
Clavius the Tribune

"I believe … I can never be the same."

If you haven't seen the 2016 film *Risen*, starring Joseph Fiennes, do yourself a favor and get a copy. It may seem odd to choose a fictional film character for this week's brother, but once you see the film, I think you'll agree it makes sense. Clavius' story helps us grasp the intimacy of being in relationship with God.

The film is a biblical drama about the Resurrection, told through the eyes of Clavius, a powerful Roman tribune in Jerusalem, charged by Pilate with the responsibility of solving the mystery of Jesus' death. In the beginning of the film, Pilate questions Clavius about his somber mood. He wonders why Clavius has such a downtrodden disposition. After all, as a tribune, he has a bright future ahead of him in the Roman army. Clavius tells Pilate he is tired and would just like to get through one day without seeing death.

Clavius eventually meets the resurrected Christ. Clavius is extremely challenged by Christ because he was present at Calvary, watching as Jesus died on the cross. So he doesn't quite know what to make of it when the man he saw perish on Golgotha is now sitting — alive — right in front of him. He's not so sure about this "God" thing, either, until Jesus asks him in a private conversation: "What is it you seek, Clavius? Certainty, peace, a day without death?"

How could Jesus have known Clavius' heart unless he were truly the Son of God?

This conversation with the Lord clinches it for Clavius. This is where he realizes who God is: an all-knowing, omnipotent, loving God. Clavius comes to understand just how up close and personal God is with each of us, no matter what our past might hold.

God knows your heart and all your struggles, cares, hurts, dreams, and desires. If you take the time to connect with him more, no doubt you will have many Clavius moments throughout your life. You will see God working in situations where you never saw him before.

In Scripture there are many verses where God says to turn and rely on him — especially in times of trouble. In 1 Peter 5:7 it says, "Cast all your anxieties on him, for he cares about you." Turn to God and let him be the fount of mercy and peace in your life — 24/7.

❓ Reflection Questions

1. Have you ever thought about your relationship with God in terms of a personal friendship? How would you describe your relationship with God right now?

2. Do you want to know Jesus on a personal, intimate level? Do you feel you already do? If not, what do you think might help you develop this type of relationship with him?

▶ Video Reflection

Watch and reflect on the Beyond Sunday "Up Close and Personal" video, available at **www.OSV.com/BeyondSunday**. Spend some time discussing it with your group. What did you relate to most in the video and why?

👤 Holy Habits of the Week

→ Schedule a time this week (maybe thirty minutes) to visit Jesus in Eucharistic Adoration. If you're not sure where to find adoration, check with your local parish or diocese for information on adoration times in your area.

→ Read through the spiritual works of mercy and pick one to work on this week: instructing, advising, consoling, comforting, forgiving,and bearing wrongs patiently.

→ If possible, grab some friends and family members and watch the 2016 movie *Risen* (you can learn more about it at http://sites.sonypictures.com/risen/discanddigital/). Discuss the up-close-and-personal relationships you see in the film with Jesus, Clavius, and the disciples.

✝ Closing Prayer: *Hail Mary*

Hail Mary, full of grace. The Lord is with thee.
Blessed art thou among women, and blessed is the fruit of thy womb, Jesus.
Holy Mary, Mother of God, pray for us sinners, now and at the hour of our death.
Amen.

Close the meeting with a prayer of intercession, inviting everyone to pray for the needs of their community.

. . . .

Read Chapter Six in the *Beyond Sunday* book before your next Beyond Sunday group meeting.

. . . .

Notes

_____

_____

_____

_____

Notes

The Three M's of Faith
Meeting, Mercy, and Mission

· ·

"If you knew the gift of God ... "

— JOHN 4:10

Let Us Pray

Lord, help us to discover our unique mission on this earth and to realize that you forgive us and love us, regardless of our past sins. We know that you are waiting to meet us. Give us the courage to get out of ourselves to meet you, receive your mercy, and live out the mission you have for us.

Holy Spirit Prayer

Come, Holy Spirit, fill the hearts of your faithful and kindle in us the fire of your love.

Send forth your Spirit and we shall be created.

And you shall renew the face of the earth.

Let us pray.

O God, who by the light of the Holy Spirit did instruct the hearts of the faithful,

grant that by the same Holy Spirit we may be truly wise and ever enjoy his consolations.

Through Christ our Lord. Amen.

BEYOND *Sunday* REFLECTION

Sometimes it's easy to keep God at a distance. We do it because we are afraid that really meeting him will change our life, perhaps in ways we won't like. And, in a way, that fear is true. Everything does change when you decide to make a serious commitment to God. But isn't that the truth for anything we take very seriously in our lives? Whether it be a commitment to our spouse, our children, or our careers, it takes effort, dedication, and concentration. And we do it, despite the fact that it isn't always easy. The effort and sacrifice seem natural and very acceptable. So why is there such a negative connotation when it comes to a commitment to God?

No matter what we may have to change in our lives, if we choose to commit to God, we can be fully confident that there is no reason to be afraid. God loves us enough to humble himself, to come to earth as a helpless child, and to die a terrible death on a cross. If someone loves us that intensely, doesn't it follow naturally that he can only want and do what's best for us if we allow him into our hearts?

Like the woman at the well, many times we have to hit rock bottom and get to a place where we realize what we have chosen does not make us happy or fulfilled. And also, like her, when we meet him, when we really finally say "yes," the gratitude for his mercy is so overwhelming that we can't just walk away from the meeting and say: "Nice chatting with you, Lord. See you around sometime when I need some prayers answered." Once we've really met him, we can't keep silent.

Like the Samaritan woman, each of us must respond in our own way to God's mercy. We meet him, we receive his mercy, and then it's time to get busy in the mission field, wherever God places us. The gift of God, his unfathomable love, is what compelled the woman at the well, and it is what drives all of us who decide we really want to meet Jesus.

***Catechism* Connection**

"The faithful, who by Baptism are incorporated into Christ and integrated into the People of God, are made sharers in their particular way in the priestly, prophetic, and kingly office of Christ, and have their own part to play in the mission of the whole Christian people in the Church and in the World." (CCC 897)

This Week's "Beyond Sunday" Sister

Saint Teresa of Calcutta

"We ourselves feel that what we are doing is just a drop in the ocean.
But the ocean would be less because of that missing drop."

Mother Teresa, now Saint Teresa of Calcutta, was propelled into her mission of service to the poor because of a special meeting. It occurred on a train ride in September 1946, when she was traveling from Calcutta to a convent in Darjeeling, India. The special meeting is what she referred to as her "call within a call." She was already a nun serving with the Sisters of Loreto congregation, but she had become very disturbed by the extreme poverty around her in India. During that train ride, she could not help but see the misery of the local people, and she felt God was calling her to serve his people differently.

She would later say, "God was calling me to give up all and to surrender myself to him in the service of the poorest of the poor in the slums."

After that meeting, and after many months of discernment with her religious superiors, she left her position at the Loreto school, resolving not only to serve the poorest of the poor, but also to live among them while doing so.

No doubt, had Mother Teresa stayed with the Sisters of Loreto, she would have led a faithful and fruitful life. But think about what the world would be like if she had not answered that call within the call of serving the poorest of the poor. There are now close to five thousand religious sisters in the Missionaries of Charity, the religious order founded by Mother Teresa to serve the poorest of the poor all over the world. They care for refugees, the mentally ill, people with AIDS, lepers, former prostitutes, and many more. They also have established schools, have set up soup kitchens, and provide other services based on the needs of the community. These services are provided without charge to anyone — no matter his or her religion or state in life.

Never underestimate what God can do in your life if you open your heart and follow him. Pray, listen, and follow your heart and trust in him. He will lead you to the life-giving water and help you find your mission in this world.

❓ Reflection Questions

1. How (and where or through whom) have you "met" Christ in your life?

2. If you have never really met him in a personal way, where do you think he might be inviting you to that face-to-face, heart-to-heart meeting? Have you been avoiding it?

3. How has God shown you mercy, and how have you responded to that mercy?

4. Do you think God has a specific mission for you? What might that be?

▶ Video Reflection

Watch and reflect on the Beyond Sunday "The Three M's of Faith" video, available at **www.OSV.com /BeyondSunday**. Spend some time discussing it with your group. What did you relate to most in the video and why?

👤 Holy Habits of the Week

This week, take your first step in evangelization. Here are some ideas:

➜ Invite someone to Mass.

➜ Send a family member or friend an email or text letting them know you were praying for them at Mass.

➜ Set a daily alarm on your phone to ring at 3:00 p.m. to remind you of the Hour of Mercy. Then pray, "Jesus, I trust in You."

➜ Make some time this week to pray the Divine Mercy Chaplet. (You can learn more about the Chaplet at http://www .usccb.org/beliefs-and-teachings /how-we-teach/new-evangelization /year-of-faith/how-to-pray-the-chaplet-of-divine-mercy.cfm)

✝ Closing Prayer: *Prayer of Saint Francis*

Lord, make me an instrument of thy peace:
Where there is hatred, let me sow love.
Where there is injury, pardon,
Where there is doubt, faith,
Where there is despair, hope that where there are shadows, I may bring light;
Where there is darkness, light,
and where there is sadness, joy.

O Divine Master, grant that I may not so much to be consoled, as to console;
To be understood, as to understand;
To be loved, as to love;
For it is in giving that we receive,.
It is in pardoning that we are pardoned
And it is by dying that we are born to eternal life.

Close the meeting with a prayer of intercession, inviting everyone to pray for the needs of their community.

· ·

Read Chapter Seven in the *Beyond Sunday* book before your next Beyond Sunday group meeting.

· ·

Notes

Five Cures for the Common Catholic Cold

"But seek first the kingdom of God and his righteousness, and all these things will be added to you."

— MATTHEW 6:33

Let Us Pray

Lord, set our faith on fire. Where we have let our faith grow weak and sick, help us take the necessary steps to find healing so that we can grow in faith and in our relationship with Jesus.

Holy Spirit Prayer

Come, Holy Spirit, fill the hearts of your faithful and kindle in us the fire of your love.

Send forth your Spirit and we shall be created.

And you shall renew the face of the earth.

Let us pray.

O God, who by the light of the Holy Spirit did instruct the hearts of the faithful,

grant that by the same Holy Spirit we may be truly wise and ever enjoy his consolations.

Through Christ our Lord. Amen.

BEYOND *Sunday* REFLECTION

It's really not rocket science. Given all the resources that are now available, including Catholic radio and TV, websites, blogs, Bible studies, and a variety of other study programs, not to mention countless conferences and retreats, we don't really have any excuses for not growing in our faith. But it all has to start somewhere, and that means taking that very first step.

You're already well on your way. Hopefully, as you have read the *Beyond Sunday* book and worked through this study guide with your group, you've experienced some real "aha" moments with God. That's a wonderful grace, and you will want to remember those experiences. These are what we call "mountaintop" experiences, and they can be really exciting.

However, you also need to come down from the mountain and live your faith in the everyday. That can get tough. It's all too easy to fall back into weak efforts and a sickly faith — the "common Catholic cold." To protect yourself from this pesky illness, you'll want to take preventive measures to avoid falling prey to sickness of the heart or spirit. Think of the five simple cures outlined in Chapter Seven of the *Beyond Sunday* book as the spiritual version of getting your flu shot or eating homemade chicken soup. Whatever might be ailing you, those five cures can be a big help in getting you back to health.

You will probably find, as you continue to grow in your faith, that you'll need to focus on different cures at different times. Sometimes you'll want to work on giving God control over your life; other times you'll probably find you need to give more attention to silence. The important thing is to stay aware, so you can make any adjustments that are needed when you start to notice your spiritual health sliding. Ask the Holy Spirit to let you know where you should be focusing your energy at any given time!

 ## *Catechism* **Connection**

"The habitual difficulty in prayer is distraction. It can affect words and their meaning in vocal prayer; it can concern, more profoundly, him to whom we are praying, in vocal prayer (liturgical or personal), meditation, and contemplative prayer. To set about hunting down distractions would be to fall into their trap, when all that is necessary is to turn back to our heart: for a distraction reveals to us what we are attached to, and this humble awareness before the Lord should awaken our preferential love for him and lead us resolutely to offer him our heart to be purified. Therein lies the battle, the choice of which master to serve." (CCC 2729)

This Week's "Beyond Sunday" Sister

Emmy-award-winning actress Patricia Heaton

"Do not be conformed to this world but be transformed by the renewal of your mind, that you may prove what is the will of God, what is good and acceptable and perfect." — ROMANS 12:2

According to a recent article on ChurchPop, Patricia Heaton was raised in a devout Catholic home where she attended daily Mass with her mom. Her sister became a Dominican nun. When Heaton was only twelve years old, her mother died of an aneurysm. This caused her to struggle for many years with depression, and at one point she even considered suicide.

"I'd sit in my apartment on the Upper West Side," she later explained, "and call on the saints, including Patrick and Joseph, for help."

Heaton left the Catholic Church following her divorce and went through a period of spiritual wilderness. It was during this time that Heaton realized that acting had become an "idol" for her. She wanted to make a change. As she later said, "I needed to put Christ first."

God eventually led her to a Catholic priest who helped guide her through the annulment process. Since then, she has been a practicing Catholic. "It was a great joy," she says of her return to her Catholic faith, "a beautiful thing."

Heaton is best known for her Emmy Award-winning role as Debra Barone in *Everybody Loves Raymond* and plays the role of Frankie Heck on the ABC original comedy *The Middle*. Heaton actively speaks out about her faith, especially on the issues of life and religious liberty. If you follow her on Twitter, you will see firsthand how she is using the power of the media for good to share Christ in this hurting world.

Patricia Heaton is a wonderful modern-day example of how to recover from a case of the common Catholic cold, or even something more serious on a spiritual level. Heaton fell away from her faith, but did not give up. She sought a cure because deep down she knew something was not quite right. The steps she took were exactly what the doctor ordered. She went to speak with someone knowledgeable and acted on his advice, eventually finding her way back home to the Church.

But she didn't stop there. It's easy to see the challenges we all face in today's world that is often hostile to people of faith. With that in mind, think about the challenges Heaton faces in the world of Hollywood. Despite those challenges, she remains strong and healthy in her faith, by speaking the truth in love, especially when it comes to causes she holds near and dear to her heart.

For all of us, putting Christ first, as Patricia Heaton learned to do, is critical for warding off the common Catholic cold, healing from other ailments we might have come down with over the years, and becoming spiritually healthy. When we put Jesus first, practicing the "five cures for the common Catholic cold" gets easier and easier. And, if we let it, it can transform our lives.

❓ Reflection Questions

1. Among the cures for the common Catholic cold, which do you find most challenging?

2. Are there aspects of your faith life where you're realizing you have developed a bit of a cold without realizing it?

3. What other "cures" do you think could help you keep your faith life alive and healthy?

▶ Video Reflection

Watch and reflect on the Beyond Sunday "Five Cures for the Common Catholic Cold" video, available at **www.OSV.com /BeyondSunday**. Spend some time discussing it with your group. What did you relate to most in the video and why?

👤 Holy Habits of the Week

→ Most adults spend about as much time connected to some sort of media as they do on the job each week. Make a commitment to cut back on your media usage this week, and use the extra time to read Scripture or to sit quietly and listen to what the Lord is trying to say to you.

→ Print out the list of the beatitudes in Matthew 5:3–12, and tape them to the mirror in your bathroom. Read through them while brushing your teeth, and ask God which one he would like you to focus on practicing each day.

✝ Closing Prayer: *Saint Michael the Archangel Prayer*

St. Michael, the Archangel, defend us in battle; be our defense against the wickedness and snares of the devil. May God rebuke him, we humbly pray; and do thou, O Prince of the heavenly host, by the power of God, thrust into hell Satan and the other evil spirits who prowl about the world seeking the ruin of souls. Amen.

Close the meeting with a prayer of intercession, inviting everyone to pray for the needs of their community.

. . . .
Read Chapter Eight in the *Beyond Sunday* book before your next Beyond Sunday group meeting.
. . . .

Notes

"God Gives Us What We Need Wrapped in What We Want"

"Take delight in the LORD, / and he will give you the desires of your heart."

— PSALMS 37:4

Let Us Pray

Lord, help us realize the difference between needs and wants. Help us to find your good gifts in unexpected places. Let us grow in virtue and love, turn away from our sins, and become the people you created us to be.

Holy Spirit Prayer

Come, Holy Spirit, fill the hearts of your faithful and kindle in us the fire of your love.

Send forth your Spirit and we shall be created.

And you shall renew the face of the earth.

Let us pray.

O God, who by the light of the Holy Spirit did instruct the hearts of the faithful,

grant that by the same Holy Spirit we may be truly wise and ever enjoy his consolations.

Through Christ our Lord. Amen.

BEYOND *Sunday* REFLECTION

"Delight in the LORD." These four words are the most important in this beautiful verse from the Book of Psalms. Often, we treat God like a slot machine. How many of us can really say we "delight" in him? Instead, we focus on other things that we think will delight us, and we focus on putting in our "tokens" — such as Mass or a few Hail Marys and Our Fathers — here and there to get us what we want.

Yet as we grow in our relationship with God, we discover that he's not just there to give us good things if we ask him hard enough. He's our Father, our savior, and our friend. As long as we keep our eyes focused on Christ and as long as we trust and remember all the great ways he has already revealed his love in our lives, we will find peace in resting in him. He truly becomes our greatest delight.

God's got this. Let's delight in the fact that he is God and we are not. We keep on keeping on through trust, through prayer, through further study, and by putting one foot in front of another. At the same time, we allow God to be God and watch him, sooner or later, give us what we need wrapped in what we want. In other words, we'll realize how he is continually granting those "desires of our hearts."

 Catechism Connection

"God created man a rational being, conferring on him the dignity of a person who can initiate and control his own actions. 'God willed that man should be "left in the hand of his own counsel," so that he might of his own accord seek his Creator and freely attain his full and blessed perfection by cleaving to him.'" (CCC 1730)

This Week's "Beyond Sunday" Brother

Jesuit Father Pedro Arrupe (1907–91)

Father Pedro Arrupe, S.J., was a Jesuit priest who served as the twenty-eighth superior general of the Jesuit order, also known as the Society of Jesus, from 1965 to 1983. He is known for his ministry to victims impacted by the atomic bomb in Hiroshima, where he applied his medical and spiritual background to serve those in need. He also was involved in leading the Jesuits in their implementation of the documents of the Catholic Church's Second Vatican Council. Father Arrupe was much loved for his spiritual approach of finding and seeing God in all things.

He composed a beautiful poem, "Fall in Love," which describes our search for the things we long for most. It offers great direction on how we discover or rediscover the deepest desires or longings of our hearts.

Sometimes, when we think of finding those deepest desires, it can be truly challenging. That's why Father Arrupe's poem is a great resource for self-reflection. It's challenging, but in many ways it's also simple. If we want to connect with those longings or desires of our hearts, we need to, as Father Arrupe says, "fall in love." More specifically, we need to fall in love with God. He created us. He knows the desires of our hearts — after all, he put them there to lead us ultimately to find our greatest joy in him.

Fall in Love

By Father Pedro Arrupe, S.J.

Nothing is more practical than
finding God, than
falling in Love
in a quite absolute, final way.
What you are in love with,
what seizes your imagination, will affect everything.
It will decide
what will get you out of bed in the morning,
what you do with your evenings,
how you spend your weekends,
what you read, whom you know,
what breaks your heart,
and what amazes you with joy and gratitude.
Fall in Love, stay in love,
and it will decide everything.

❓ Reflection Questions

1. What does the phrase "God gives us what we need wrapped in what we want" mean to you in your life right now?

2. How do you see what or whom you love impacting what you truly need and want?

3. Are there any wants you might be keeping away from God because you think he won't fulfill them — or that his wants will somehow get in the way of yours? How can you let God into the desires of your heart?

4. Are there things you want right now that might be in conflict with your true needs?

▶ Video Reflection

Watch and reflect on the Beyond Sunday "God Gives Us What We Need Wrapped in What We Want" video, available at **www.OSV.com/BeyondSunday**. Spend some time discussing it with your group. What did you relate to most in the video and why?

🧑 Holy Habits of the Week

→ Spend some time reflecting on the desires of your heart. What are the things you want most? Make a list of these desires and bring them to prayer. Invite God to be part of your whole life — including the things you long for the most.

→ Sometimes giving up little things we like can help us know our deeper desires better and to understand how God is trying to speak to us in our everyday lives. Consider what you can fast from each Friday in thanksgiving to Jesus for dying on the cross for you. You might even want to offer this up for a friend or family member in need. Some ideas of ways to "fast":

- Don't put the radio on in the car so that you can pray.
- Skip the cream and sugar in your coffee.
- Omit the salad dressing.
- Drink water instead of soda or wine.
- Spend less time on social media and replace that time with a prayer for a friend.

✝ Closing Prayer: *Glory Be*

Glory be to the Father, and to the Son, and to the Holy Spirit.
As it was in the beginning, is now, and ever shall be, world without end. Amen.

Close the meeting with a prayer of intercession, inviting everyone to pray for the needs of their community.

• •

Read the Epilogue and Resources in the *Beyond Sunday* book before your next group meeting.

• •

Notes

Notes

So Now What?

Read the Epilogue and the Resources section of the Beyond Sunday *book and discuss the following section with your group.*

Let Us Pray

Lord, guide us in our efforts to seek the truth, using the many Catholic resources available to us.

Holy Spirit Prayer

Come, Holy Spirit, fill the hearts of your faithful and kindle in us the fire of your love.

Send forth your Spirit and we shall be created.

And you shall renew the face of the earth.

Let us pray.

O God, who by the light of the Holy Spirit did instruct the hearts of the faithful,

grant that by the same Holy Spirit we may be truly wise and ever enjoy his consolations.

Through Christ our Lord. Amen.

BEYOND *Sunday* REFLECTION

When it comes to our spiritual life and growing in faith, it's all about quality, not quantity.

You've just begun your Beyond Sunday journey, and it's important to keep this in mind as you go forward beyond this book and study series. When starting a new routine, we tend to go overboard and bite off more than we can chew. Just think about the many New Year's resolutions that have come and gone over the years. Most of the time, our fad diets fade away even before mid-January. Although we have good intentions, it is difficult to change our routine and make it consistent and long-lasting.

When considering changing the way you live your faith, be realistic. Set realistic goals and stick to them. For example, you might try reading one line of Scripture each morning and then meditating on it throughout the day. Consider writing the Scripture on a Post-it note and put it on the mirror in your bathroom or on the front of your refrigerator or microwave. If you want to learn more about what's going on in the Church today, consider reading the first three articles at the top of the *EWTN News* website (http://ewtnnews.com/) each morning.

Adopting a "quality not quantity" method in your prayer life would also be beneficial — think about this when you are setting your and spiritual reading goals and you prayer goals. Wise and holy people will tell you that praying very slowly with concentration for five minutes can be much more fruitful than praying for thirty minutes with your mind and heart wandering. If your prayer is not raising your mind and heart to God, then change what you are doing. Remember, we're looking for quality, not quantity. What's the most important quality? That's simple: love.

Catechism **Connection**

"'Prayer is the raising of one's mind and heart to God or the requesting of good things from God.' But when we pray, do we speak from the height of our pride and will, or 'out of the depths' of a humble and contrite heart? He who humbles himself will be exalted; *humility* is the foundation of prayer. Only when we humbly acknowledge that 'we do not know how to pray as we ought,' are we ready to receive freely the gift of prayer. 'Man is a beggar before God.'" (CCC 2559)

This Week's "Beyond Sunday" Sister
Saint Thérèse of Lisieux

"Miss no single opportunity of making some small sacrifice, here by a smiling look, there by a kindly word; always doing the smallest right and doing it all for love."

Saint Thérèse of Lisieux, known as The Little Flower, is one of the most beloved saints in the Church today. She is one of the great Doctors of the Church, known for her spirituality, which she called her "little way" to heaven. She did small things with great love and devotion. She reminds us that it is not great deeds that count, but great love.

Thérèse understood, and teaches us, that it is the little things that count in life. Small gestures like a smile, a pat on the shoulder, or a long hug can make all the difference in someone's day. These acts of love and sacrifice can bring spiritual beauty to others, like a blooming rose. This is why she has been known to send flowers to those who ask for her prayers or seek to follow her "little way."

Living our faith this way means everything we do can become a prayer. Maybe you're folding laundry and take the time to match up all of the socks that go together. Or perhaps you intentionally put down your smartphone while talking to a friend in person. Any of these things done with great love can make all the difference. And when our whole life is made up of these kinds of actions, it can change the world.

❓ Reflection Questions

1. What are your goals for your spiritual life now that you've completed this Beyond Sunday study? What are the one or two areas in your life where you want to focus on making small changes every day?

2. Do you believe that it's really about quality, not quantity? What are some of the doubts or concerns you have about this idea and how it could play out in your life?

3. What is one small thing you do each day that you can turn into a prayer by "infusing" some love into it?

👤 Holy Habits of the Week

➜ Make a media plan and put time limits on television or screen time. You might also impose a "no phones at the table" rule for family meals, not only for your kids, but also for yourself as well.

➜ Look at your daily routine and consider how you can add a few minutes of prayer time each day. Even if it's just five minutes, make it a priority. Set an alarm on your phone, if you need a reminder.

➜ Have you ever been on a retreat? Or has it been a long time since you attended one? Consider taking a weekend and spending some focused time in prayer, either by yourself or with others. Many groups host retreats throughout the year, and there are a number of retreat centers and monasteries that invite people to rent a room and enjoy their own private retreat. Please review the retreat centers in the resource section of the *Beyond Sunday* book. We also recommend that you check with your local diocese for retreats it may be offering in your area.

✝ Closing Prayer: *Prayers of Thanksgiving*

Say a closing prayer of thanksgiving for the study group and especially for God's constant invitation to live our lives more fully in him. Invite everyone to join in and express their gratitude to God for all of their blessings, and especially for all they have learned in this study.

Notes

Notes

About the Authors

TERESA TOMEO is a syndicated Catholic talk-show host, author of numerous books, and an international speaker. She has more than thirty years of experience in television, radio, and newspaper, twenty of which were as a secular reporter/anchor in the Detroit market. Her weekday morning radio program, *Catholic Connection*, is produced by Ave Maria Radio in Ann Arbor, Michigan, and the Eternal Word Television Network, now heard on more than 500 radio stations worldwide, and on the internet through the EWTN Global Catholic Radio Network. Teresa is a columnist and special correspondent for the national Catholic newspaper *OSV Newsweekly* and appears frequently on the EWTN Global Catholic Television Network. She co-hosts the EWTN television series *The Catholic View for Women* and is a field reporter for its annual March for Life coverage in Washington, D.C. Teresa has been featured on *The O'Reilly Factor, Fox News, Fox & Friends, MSNBC, The Dr. Laura Show,* and *Dr. James Dobson's Family Talk Radio,* discussing issues of faith, media awareness, and Catholic Church teaching, especially as it relates to the culture. She gained international recognition when she spoke at a Vatican conference in 2013 hosted by the Pontifical Council for the Family. She also hosts a monthly webinar, *Catholic Leaders Webinar Series: Media Matters,* produced by Our Sunday Visitor. Teresa owns her own speaking and communications company, Teresa Tomeo Communications, LLC. Teresa and her husband, Deacon Dominick Pastore, live in Michigan, and speak around the world on the issue of marriage, based on their book, *Intimate Graces.* Connect with Teresa via her website/blog at www.TeresaTomeo.com, or on Facebook @MrsTeresaTomeo and on Twitter @TeresaTomeo.

GAIL CONIGLIO is a mother of three, president and founder of Gail Jean Marketing & Media, and has been working in Catholic marketing and media for more than 15 years. She earned a Bachelor of Science in Business Administration in Marketing from the University of Florida. She serves as marketing consultant, literary agent, and publicist for Father Mitch Pacwa, S.J. and Teresa Tomeo, as well as several other authors. She also serves as the director of marketing for Ignatius Productions, Father Pacwa's Jesuit Video Production apostolate, as well as for Teresa Tomeo Communications, where she specializes in evangelization through marketing and social media strategies. For over thirty years, Gail has been a small-group study leader, catechist, and RCIA teacher. She began her work in Catholic lay evangelization while serving in both the Charismatic and Cursillo movements. Gail is an active parishioner and serves in several ministries at her parish, including leading the Welcome Ministry and coordinator of several Women of Grace® study groups. She earned a certificate of evangelization from the Archdiocese of Miami. Prior to her work in Catholic media, Gail was radio host for the American Chamber of Christians in Business' Chamber Hour, worked in sales and marketing in the hospitality industry and served on the boards of directors and received numerous awards from the Hotel Sales & Marketing Association International and National Association of Catering Executives in Broward County. Connect with Gail on Twitter (@GailConiglio) and LinkedIn (www.LinkedIn.com/in/GailConiglio).

Stay Connected with "Beyond Sunday" Happenings!

Visit the Beyond Sunday website and sign up for our *Beyond Sunday* news and other resources that will help you live out and grow in your faith.

www.OSV.com/BeyondSunday

....

Host a Beyond Sunday Mission at Your Parish
Invite Teresa and Gail to do a Beyond Sunday Mission at your parish!

Send speaking inquiries and your Beyond Sunday questions, testimonies, and feedback to:

BeyondSunday@osv.com

....

Bulk orders
To place a bulk order for the
Beyond Sunday Study Guide, contact:

www.OSV.com/BeyondSundayBulkOrder

....

Special Thanks

Thank you to Greg Willits, Mary Beth Baker, and the entire Our Sunday Visitor team for their amazing support and for embracing this study to help save souls.

We would also like to extend our special thanks to Michele Chinault, study leader from Gail's parish — St. Mark the Evangelist Parish in Southwest Ranches, Florida. We appreciate her valuable and thoughtful insights for this study.

....

Dedication

We dedicate this study to the amazing "T Team" of Teresa Tomeo Communications: Marcy, Palma, Patti, Jeff, Lyn, and Liz — all inspiring examples of what it means to go "beyond Sunday" and help others do the same.